Super Safari

Activity Book

Level 3

Herbert Puchta • **Günter Gerngross** • **Peter Lewis-Jones**

T0349668

CAMBRIDGE
UNIVERSITY PRESS

Shaftesbury Road, Cambridge CB2 8EA, United Kingdom

One Liberty Plaza, 20th Floor, New York, NY 10006, USA

477 Williamstown Road, Port Melbourne, VIC 3207, Australia

314–321, 3rd Floor, Plot 3, Splendor Forum, Jasola District Centre, New Delhi – 110025, India

103 Penang Road, #05–06/07, Visioncrest Commercial, Singapore 238467

Cambridge University Press & Assessment is a department of the University of Cambridge.

We share the University's mission to contribute to society through the pursuit of education, learning and research at the highest international levels of excellence.

www.cambridge.org
Information on this title: www.cambridge.org/9781107477087

First published 2015

40 39 38 37 36 35 34 33

Printed in Malaysia by Vivar Printing

A catalogue record for this publication is available from the British Library

ISBN   978-1-107-47708-7   Activity Book Level 3
ISBN   978-1-107-47707-0   Pupil's Book with DVD-ROM Level 3
ISBN   978-1-107-47709-4   Teacher's Book Level 3
ISBN   978-1-107-47712-4   Class Audio CDs Level 3
ISBN   978-1-107-47716-2   Flashcards Level 3
ISBN   978-1-107-47720-9   Presentation Plus DVD-ROM Level 3
ISBN   978-1-107-53928-0   Big Book Level 3
ISBN   978-1-107-49664-4   Posters Level 3
ISBN   978-1-107-47732-2   Puppet

Additional resources for this publication at www.cambridge.org/supersafari

Super Safari Level 3 Activity Book

Hello!

1 Look, match and say the names.

1
2
3
4

2 **Find pairs and circle.**

1

3

4 Say the words. Colour the circles.

1

2

3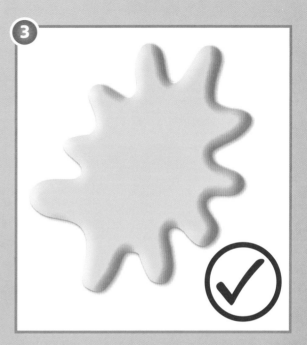

4

5

6

1 My classroom

1 Find and circle.

pencil, chair, bag, rubber, book, desk

2 **Look and count. Circle the numbers.**

	7	8	9	10
	7	8	9	10
	7	8	9	10
	7	8	9	10

3 CD1 12 Listen and circle.

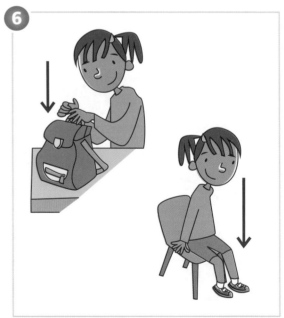

4 **Listen again. Draw and colour.**

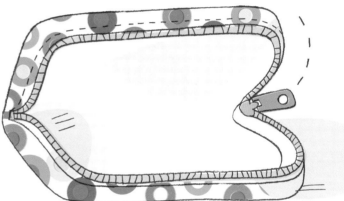

5 Look at the story. Count, match and trace the numbers.

6 Complete the faces with 😊 or ☹.

1

2

7 Make a collage.

8 Say the words. Colour the circles.

1

2

3

4

5

6

2 My family

1 Circle and say the words.

grandpa, grandma, mum, dad, sister, brother

2 CD1 23 Listen and circle.

1

2

3

4

5

6

This is my (brother). 17

Look and say the family words.

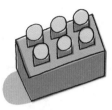

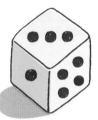

4 Point and say the names and the words.

1

2

3

4

5

6

5 Look at the story. Count and colour.

6 Complete the faces with ☺ or ☹.

1

2

7 **Make an ice lolly stick family.**

1

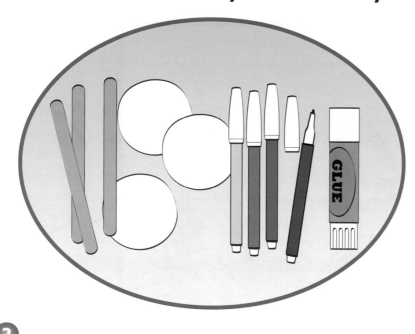 

2

3

8 **Say the words. Colour the circles.**

1

2

3

4

5

6

③ My face

1 Colour and describe one clown. Listen and colour a friend's clown.

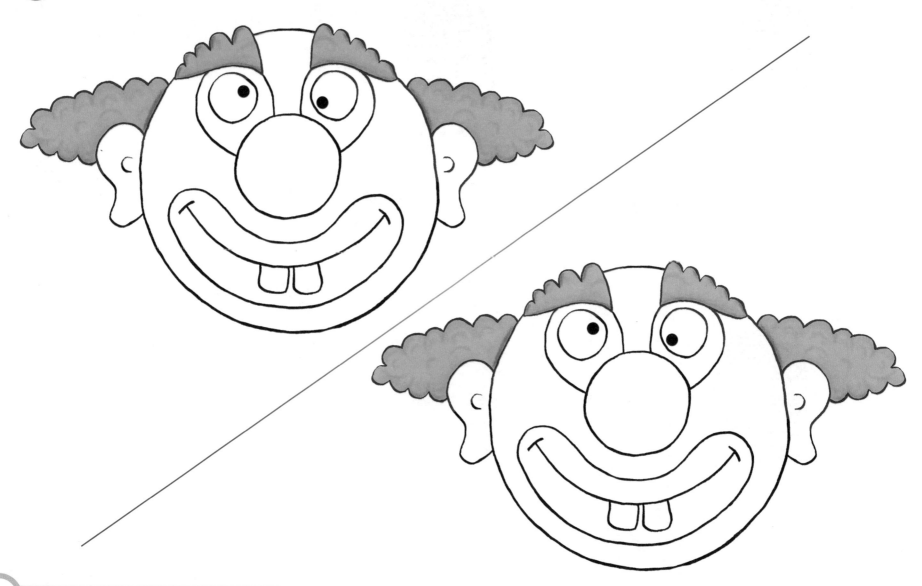

eyes, ears, nose, face, teeth, mouth

2 Look, draw and say the words.

1

2

3

4

I'm / You're (angry / happy / sad / scared). **25**

Listen and circle.

1

2

3

4

4 **Think how you are feeling today. Complete the face.**

6 Complete the faces with ☺ or ☹.

1

2

7 Make a xylophone.

1

2

8 Say the words. Colour the circles.

1

2

3

4

5

6

4 My toys

1 Count and match. Trace the numbers.

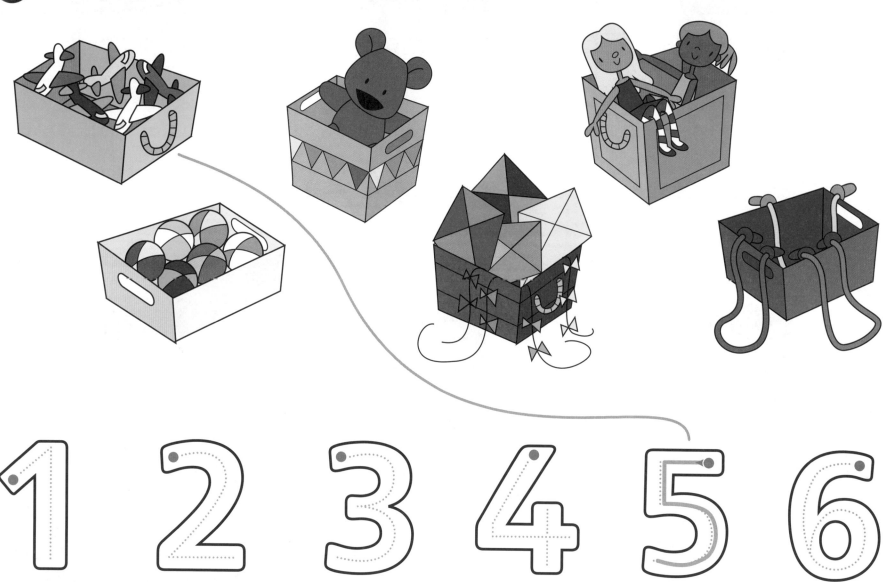

ball, kite, rope, teddy bear, doll, plane

2 **Draw and describe three toys. Listen and draw a friend's toys.**

3 Look and count. Circle the numbers.

kite	5	6	7	8	9	10
ball	5	6	7	8	9	10
doll	5	6	7	8	9	10

bear	5	6	7	8	9	10
plane	5	6	7	8	9	10
jump rope	5	6	7	8	9	10

4 Listen again. Complete the toys.

5 Look at the story. Draw the ball and the stick.

6 **Complete the faces with ☺ or ☹.**

1

2

7 Make a paper plane.

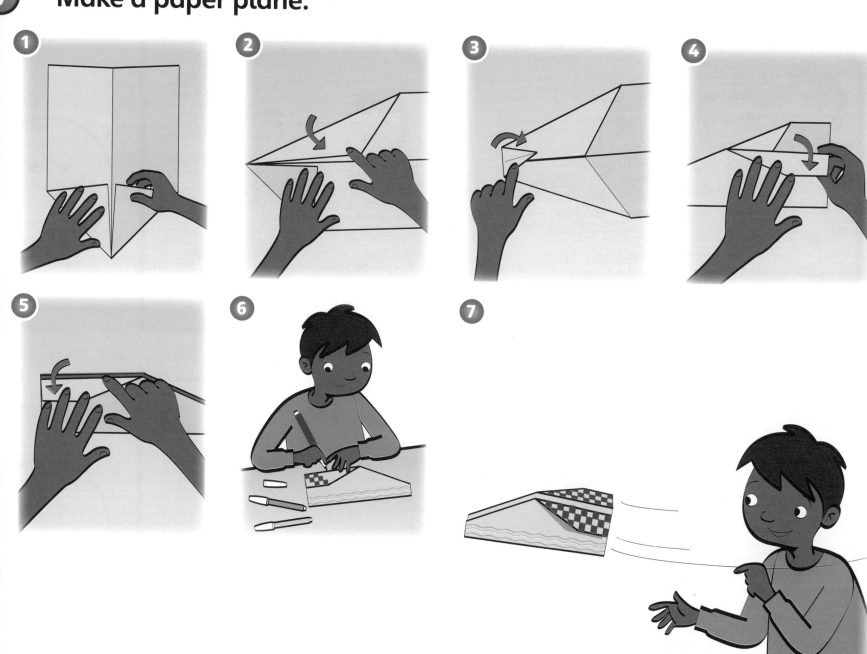

① ② ③ ④ ⑤ ⑥ ⑦

8 **Say the words. Colour the circles.**

1 kite

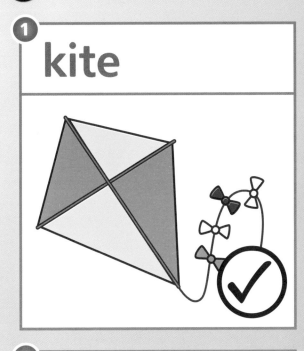

2 ball

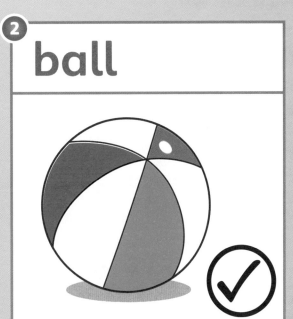

3 doll

4 teddy bear

5 plane

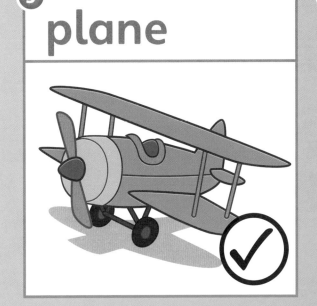

6 rope

5 My house

1 Match and say the sentences.

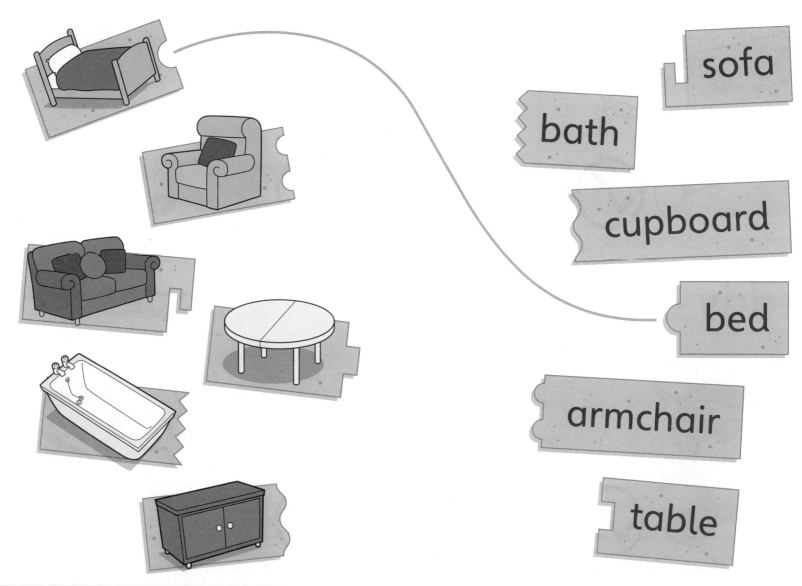

sofa

bath

cupboard

bed

armchair

table

bath, cupboard, bed, sofa, table, armchair

2 **Find the toys.**

The (doll) is (in / on / under) the (cupboard). **41**

3 Find pairs and circle.

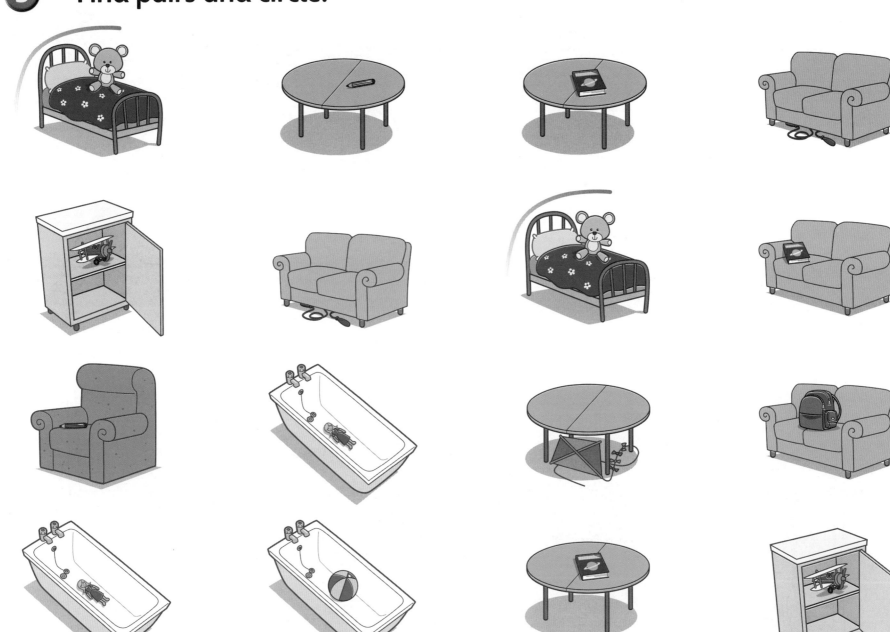

4 CD2 09 Listen and draw lines.

Look at the story. Find and say the picture number.

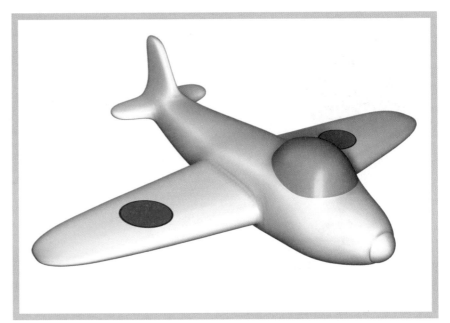

6 Complete the faces with ☺ or ☹.

1

2

7 # Make dolls' furniture.

1

2

3

4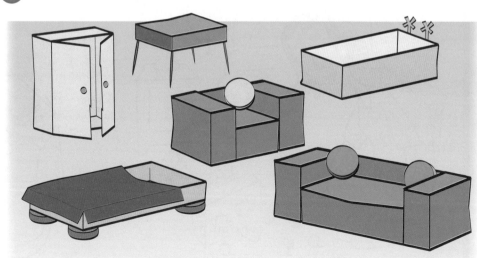

⑧ Say the words. Colour the circles.

① bed

② table

③ armchair

④ cupboard

⑤ sofa

⑥ bath

On the farm

1 Complete the animals. Say the words.

1

dog

2

cat

3

sheep

4

cow

5

rabbit

6

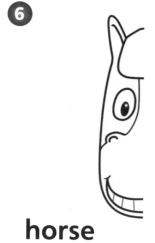

horse

cat, horse, cow, dog, rabbit, sheep

2 Talk in class and count.

3 Draw your favourite animal.

4 **Listen, point and say the words.**

5 **Remember the story. Circle the parts of the face.**

1

2

3

4

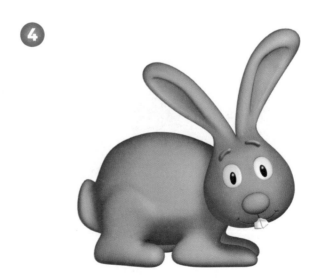

6 Complete the faces with 🙂 or 🙁.

1

2

7 Make a woolly sheep.

 **8** **Say the words. Colour the circles.**

1 dog

2 cat

3 sheep

4 cow

5 rabbit

6 horse

7 I'm hungry!

1 Look, draw and say the words.

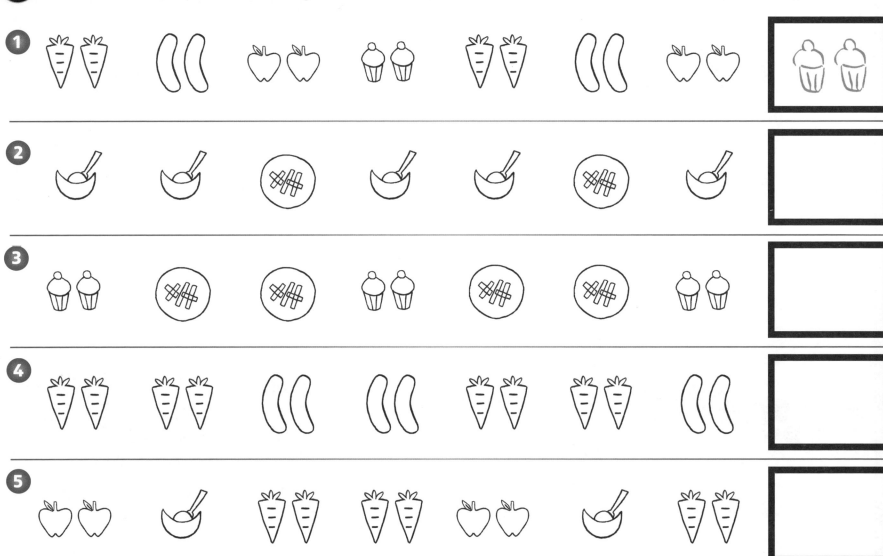

carrots, sausages, apples, cakes, ice cream, chips

2 Look and tick (✓) ♡ or ⊗. Listen to a friend and tick (✓).

Me	apples	fries	cakes	carrots	ice cream
♡					
⊗					

My friend	apples	fries	cakes	carrots	ice cream
♡					
⊗					

I like / don't like (carrots). 57

3 **Play the game.**

4 CD2 32 **Listen and draw.**

5 **Look at the story. Draw the food.**

6 Complete the faces with ☺ or ☹.

1

2

7 Make biscuit faces.

8 Say the words. Colour the circles.

1 carrots

2 sausages

3 apples

4 cakes

5 ice cream

6 chips

8 All aboard!

1 Match and say the sentences.

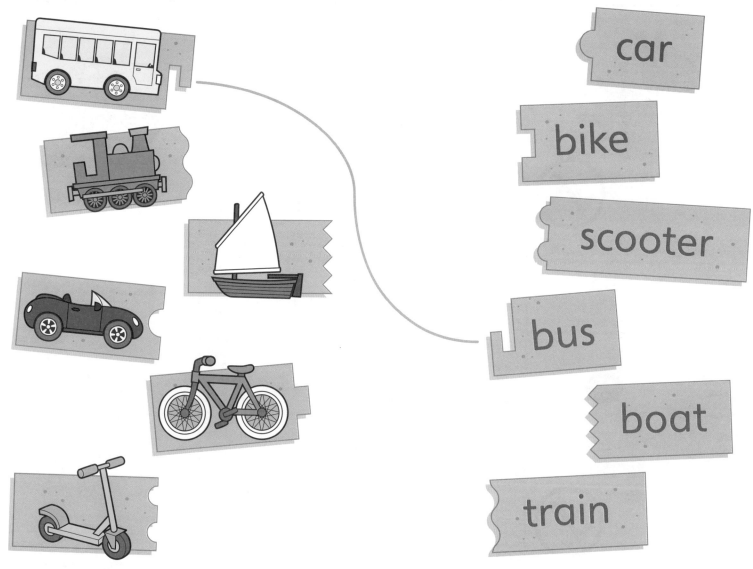

car

bike

scooter

bus

boat

train

boat, train, car, scooter, bus, bike

2 Follow the lines. Say the sentences.

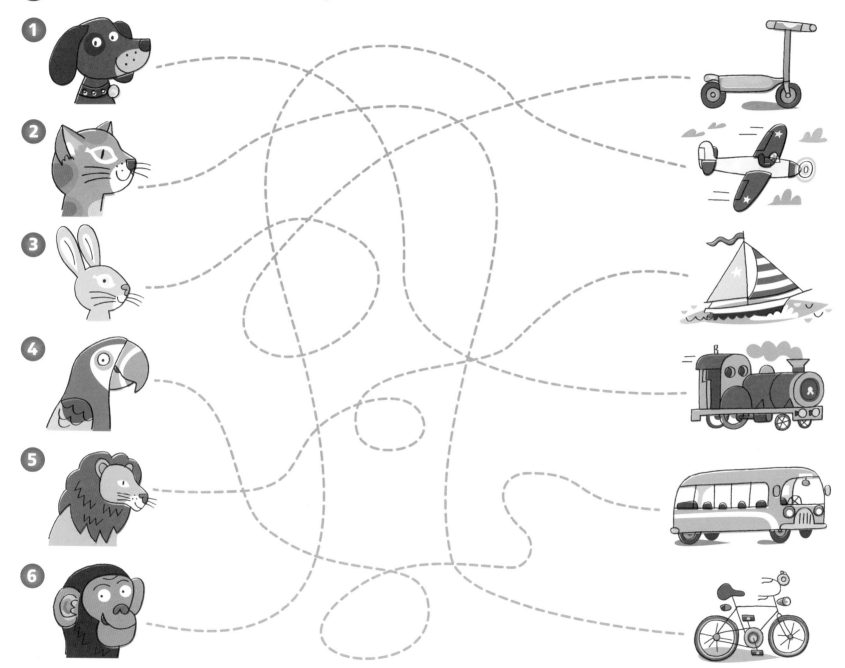

1
2
3
4
5
6

I'm / You're (riding) a (bike). 65

3 CD2 41 **Listen and circle.**

1

2

3

4

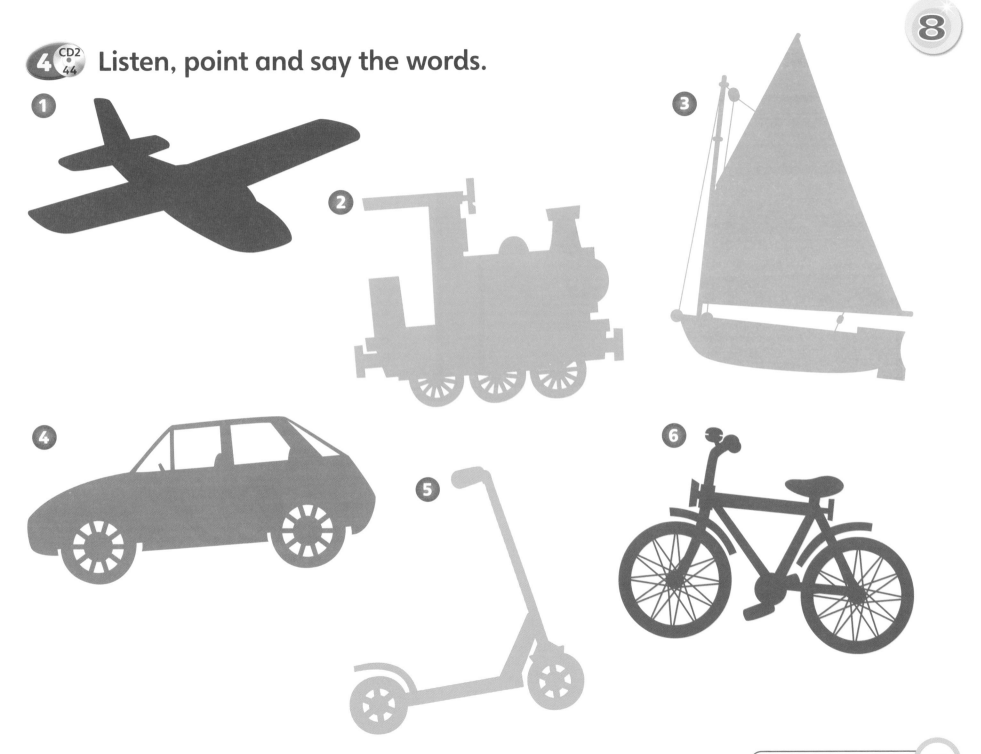

4 CD2 44 **Listen, point and say the words.**

1

2

3

4

5

6

5 **Look at the story. Draw and colour.**

6 Complete the faces with ☺ or ☹.

1

2

7 Make a boat. Have a race.

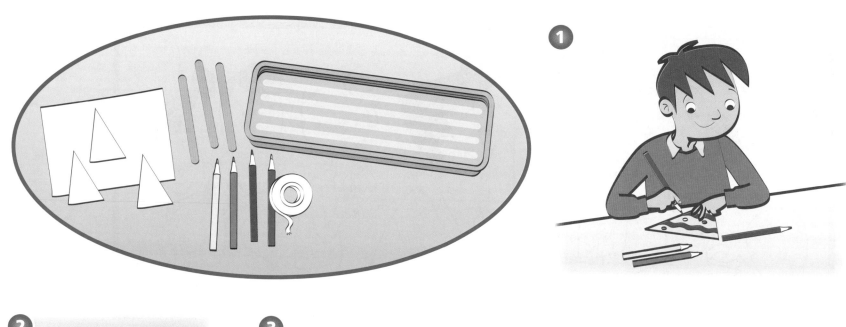

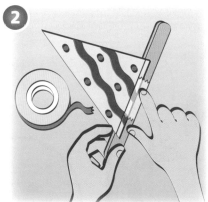

8 Say the words. Colour the circles.

1 car

2 train

3 scooter

4 bike

5 boat

6 bus

9 Party clothes

1 Draw five lines. Guess with your friend.

hat, belt, boots, shirt, badge, shoes

2 Follow the food and drink.

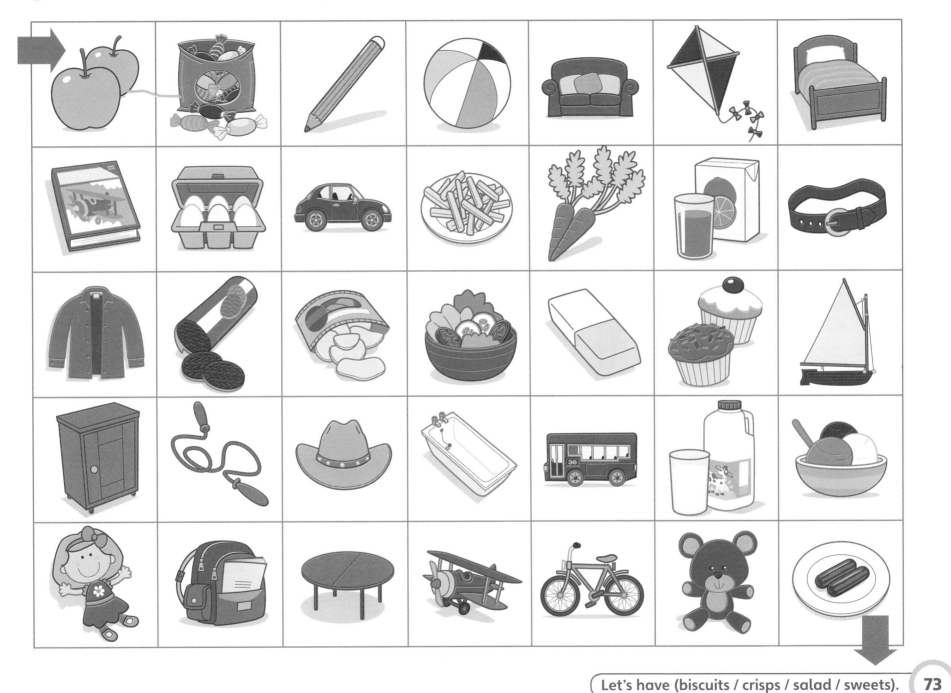

Look and circle the different picture.

1

2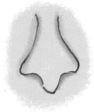

3

4

5

4 Find five differences.

1

2

5 Look at the story. Find and say the picture number.

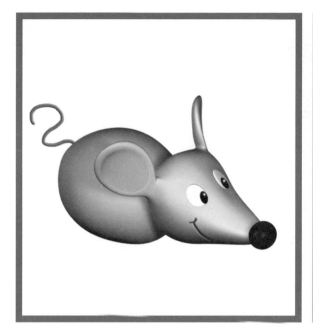

6 Complete the faces with ☺ or ☹.

1

2

7 Make a pirate hat.

8 **Say the words. Colour the circles.**

1 shirt

2 hat

3 boots

4 shoes

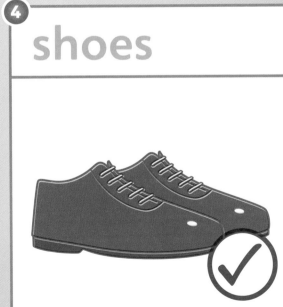

5 belt

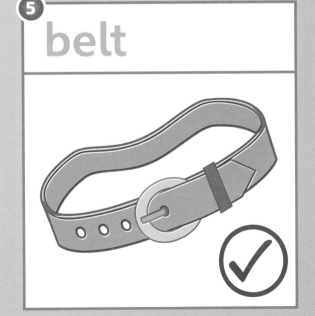

6 badge

king

cat

dancing

singing

yogurt

yellow

zoo

zebra

hat

happy

dig

dog

rabbit

red

family

fish

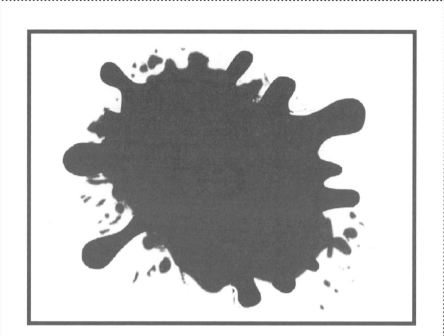

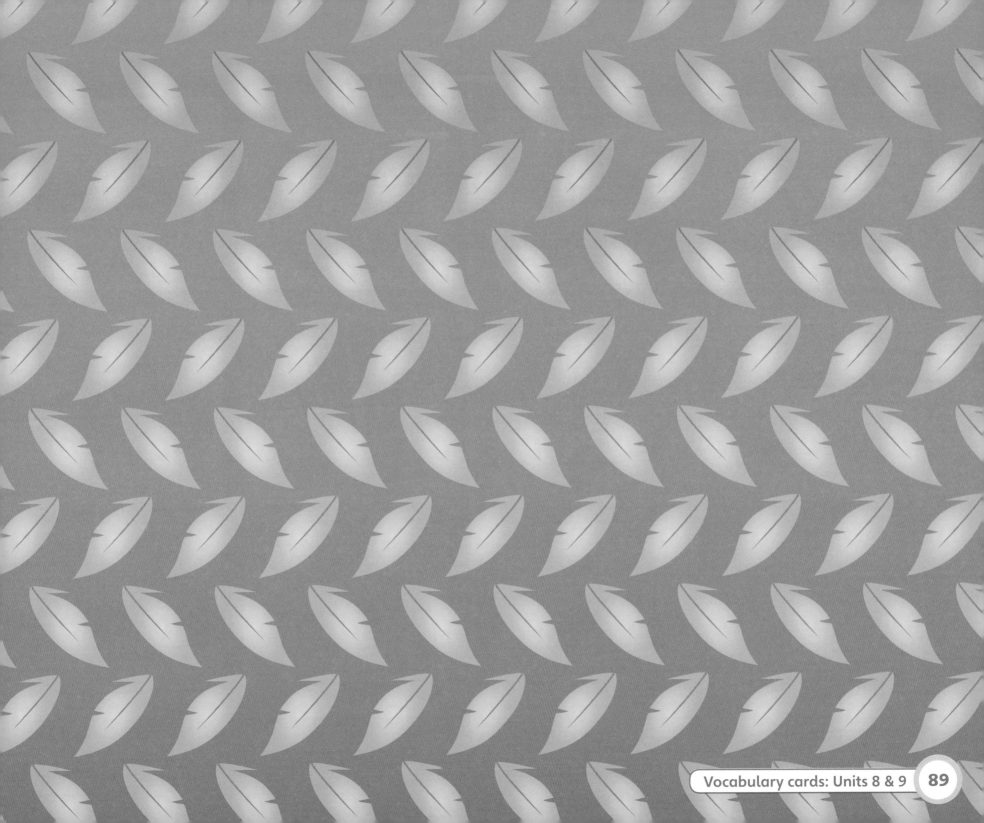

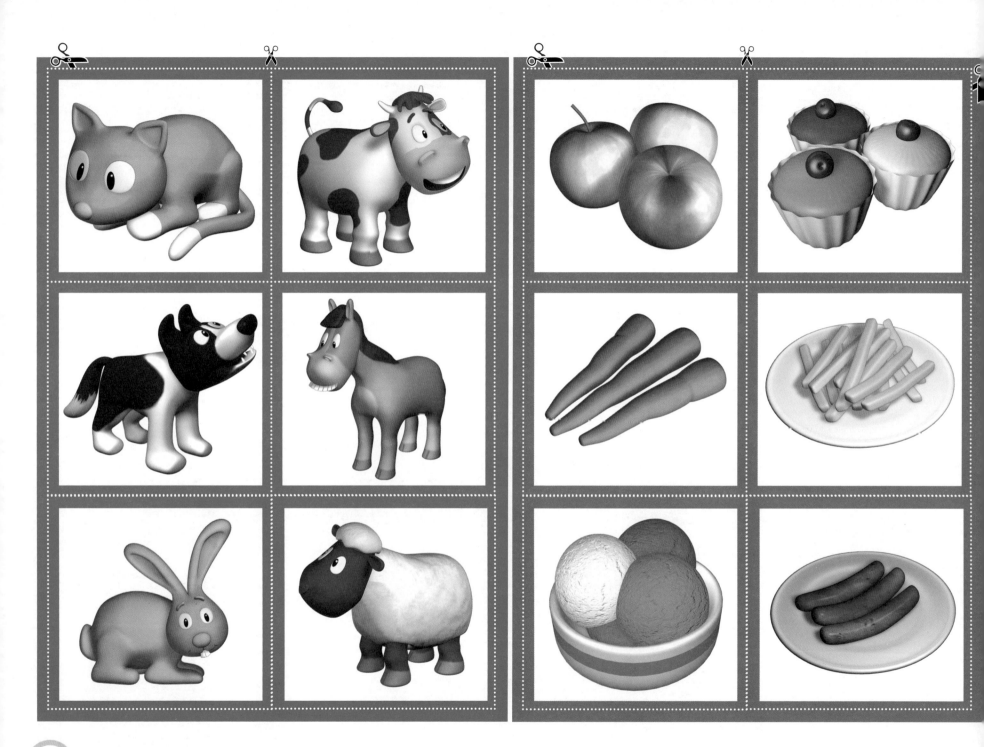

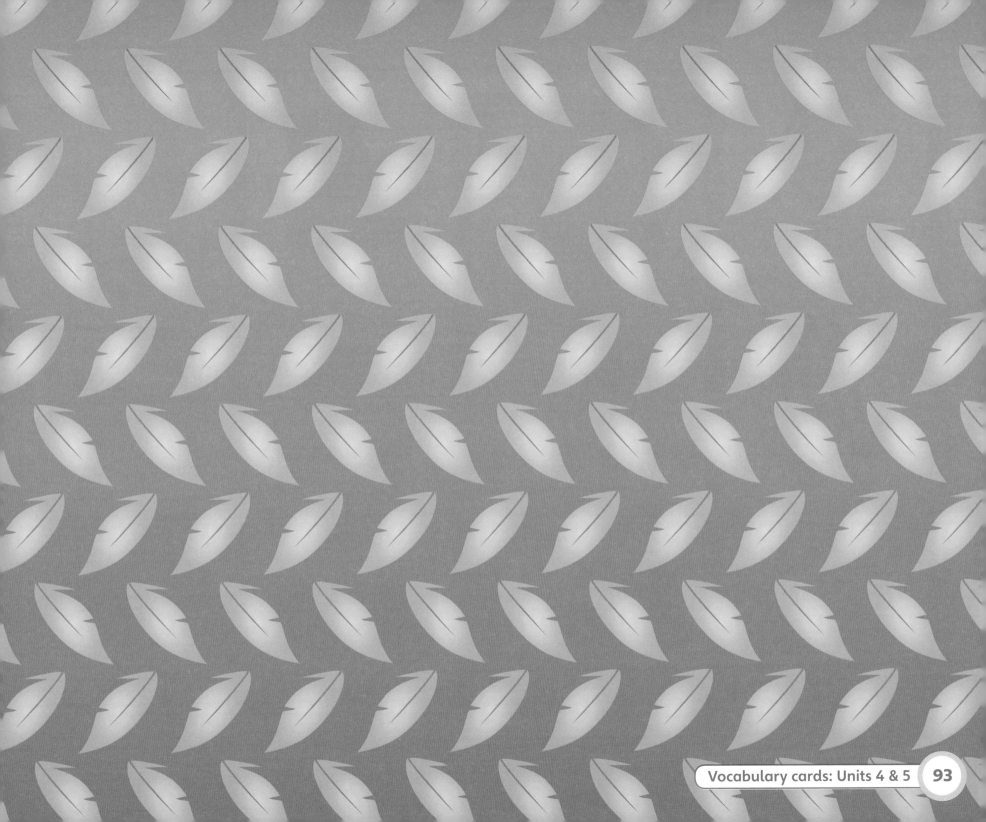

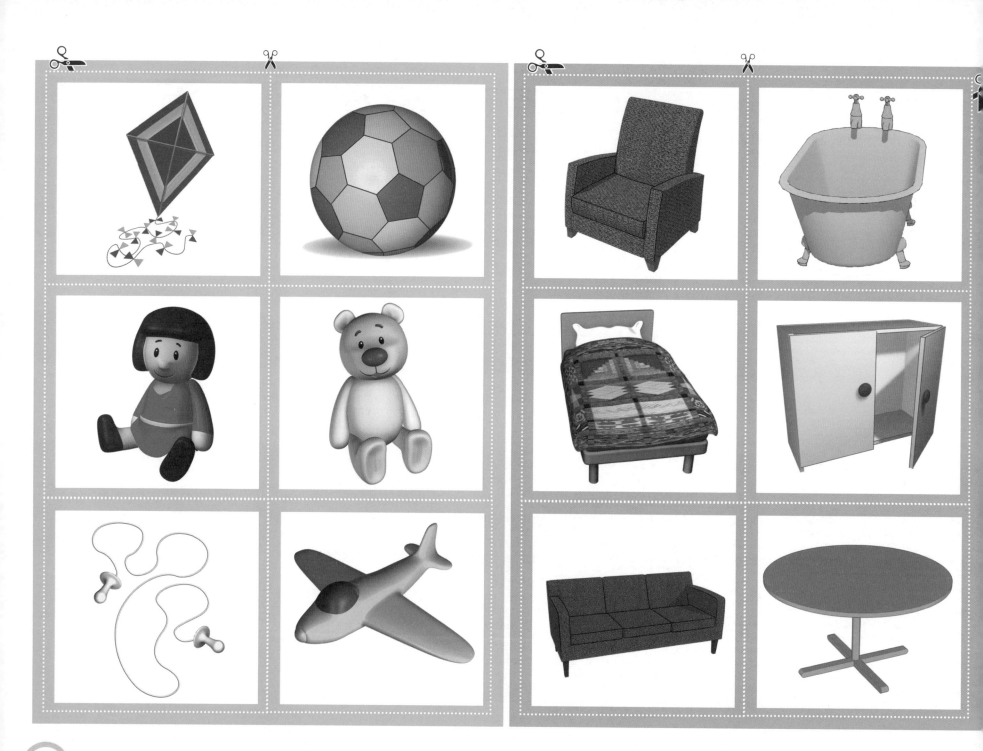

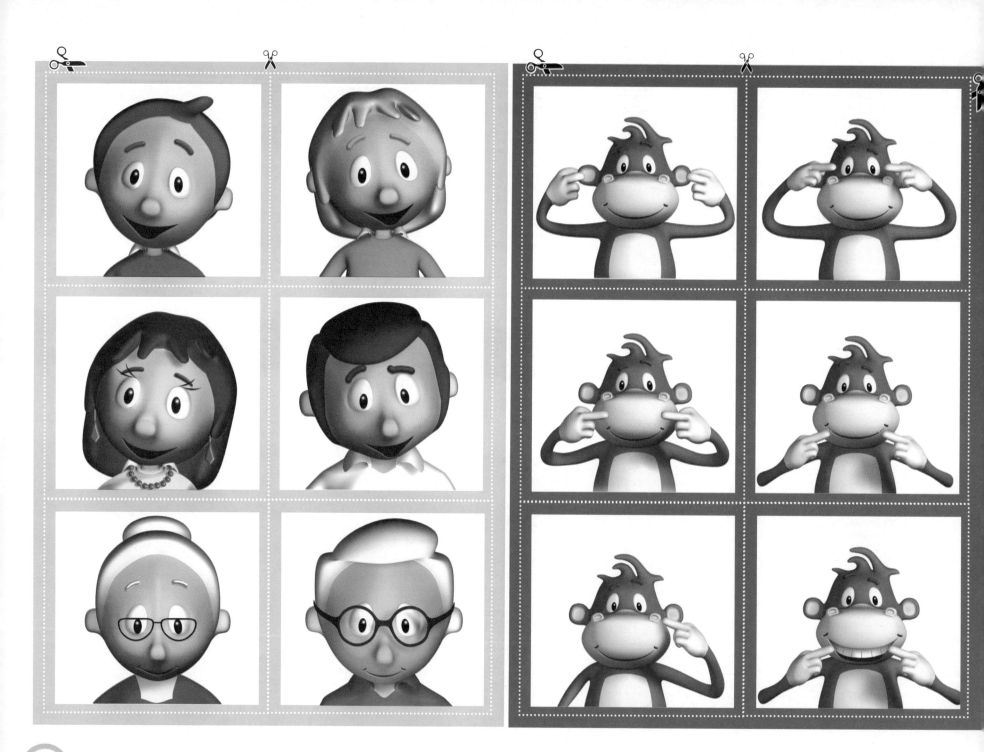

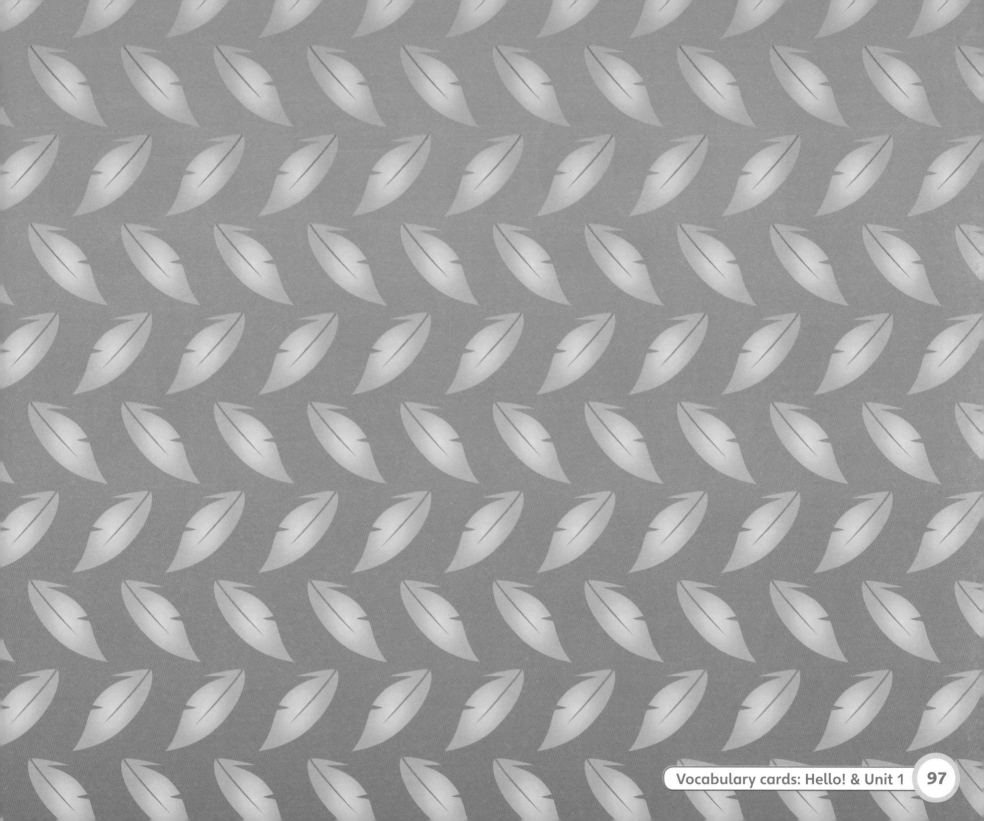

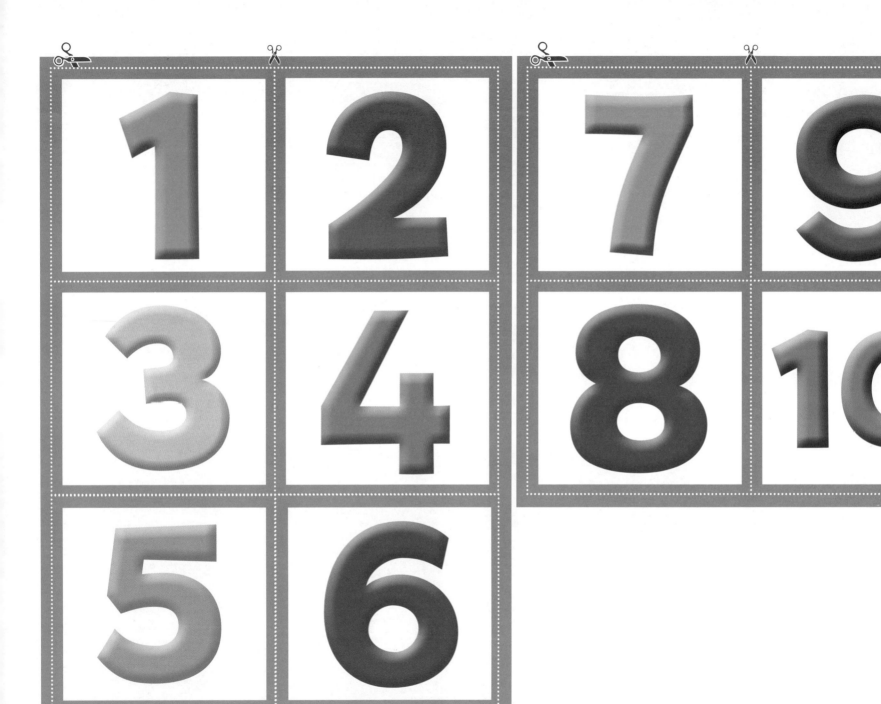

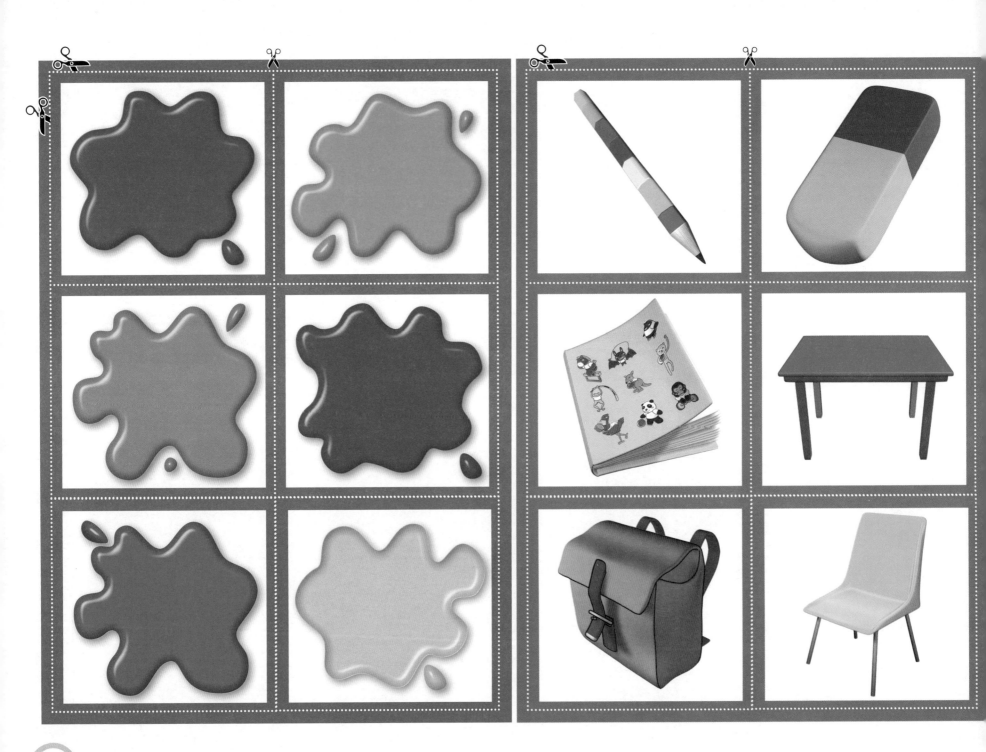

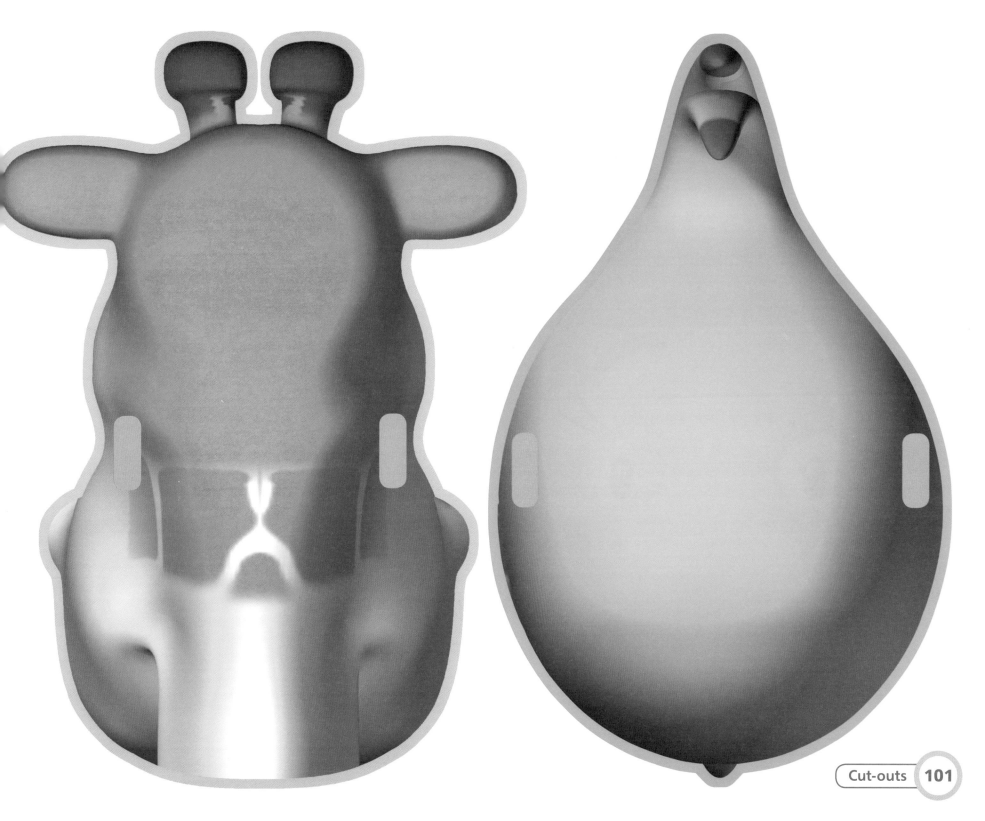

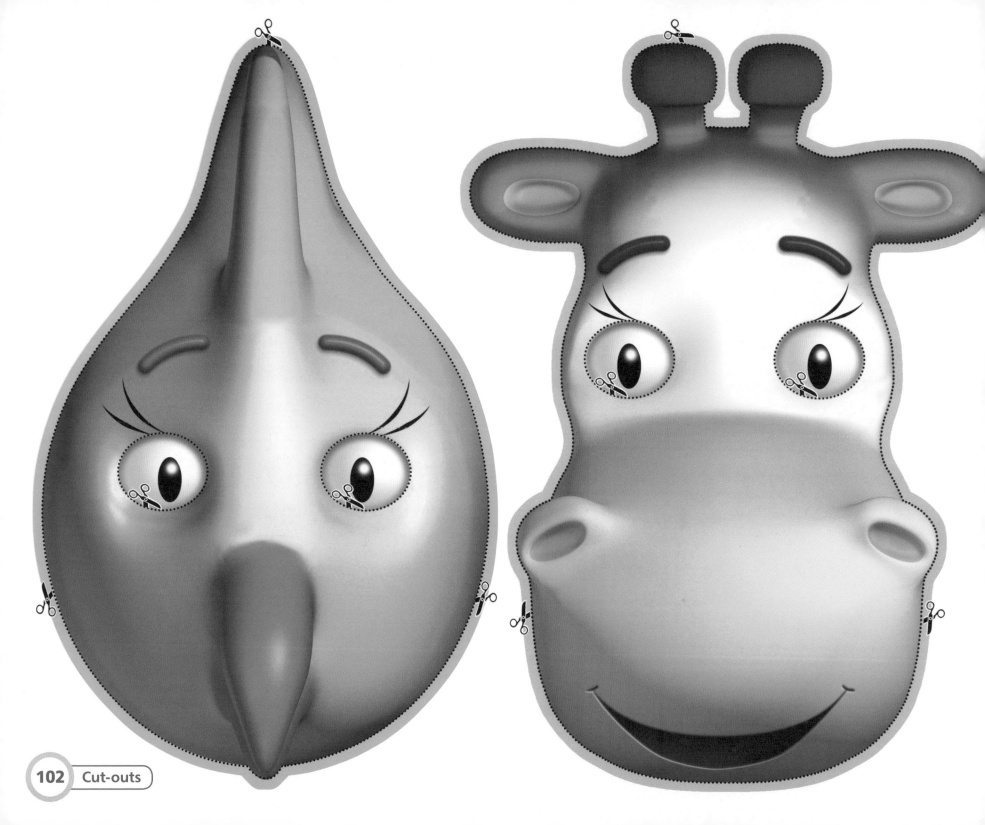

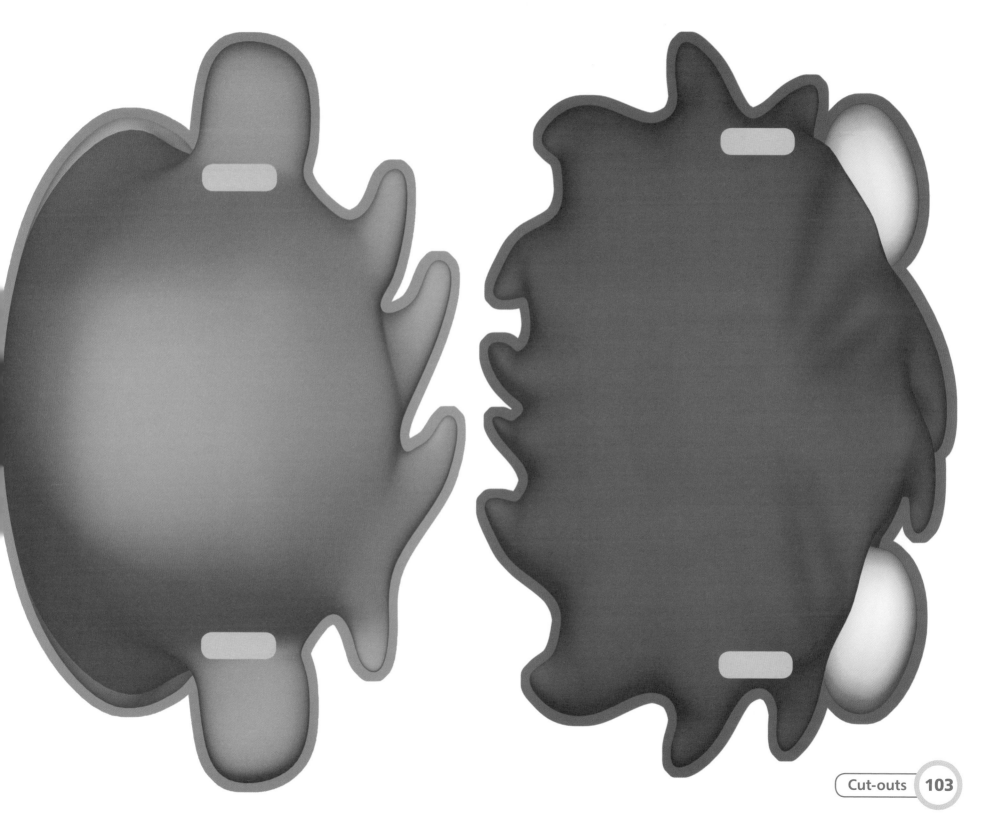

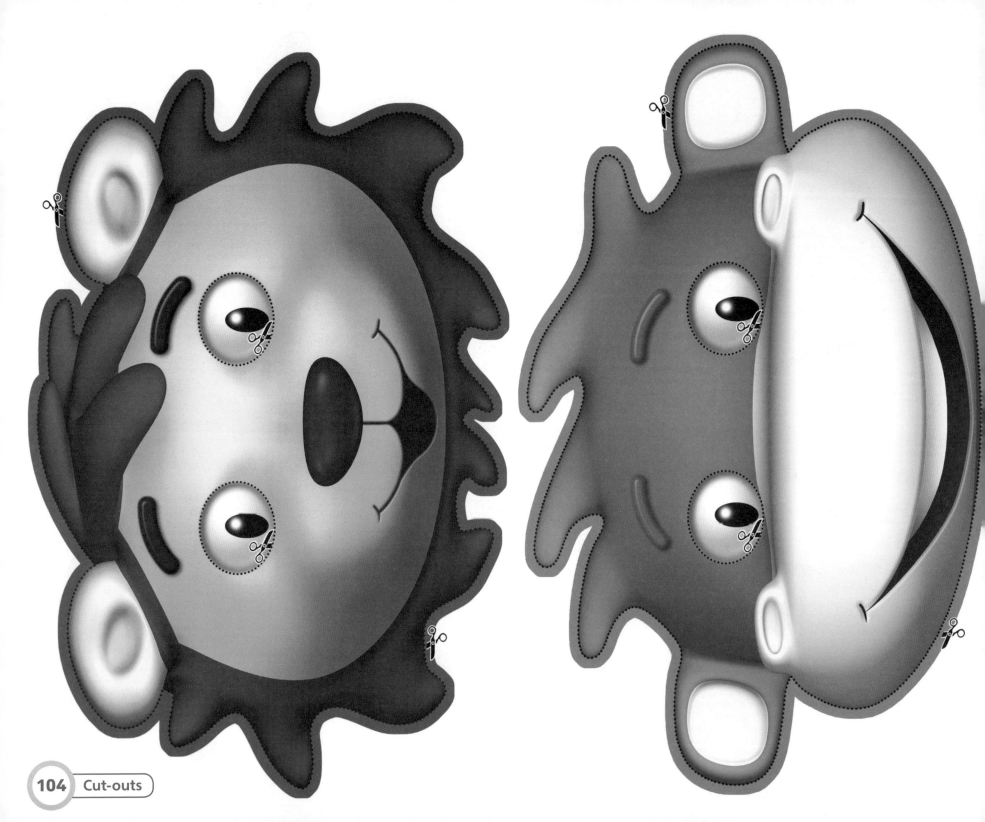